# Santa's Favorite Sports Jokes

*by Santa Claus
and His Helpers:*

**Russ Edwards and Jack Kreismer**

*Editorial:* Ellen Fischbein

*Artwork:* Jack Kreismer Sr.

*Contributor:* Angela Demers

*Cover and Page Design:*
Fred and Diane Swartz

**RED-LETTER PRESS, INC.**
Saddle River, New Jersey

**SANTA'S FAVORITE SPORTS JOKES**

Copyright © 1998 Red-Letter Press, Inc.

ISBN: 0-940462-67-2

All Rights Reserved

Printed in the United States of America

For information address Red-Letter Press, Inc.

P.O. Box 393, Saddle River, N.J. 07458

# INTRODUCTION

The elves and I can spend the entire evening surfing sports on the tube...and considering that North Pole nights are six months long, you know we have to be true fans! Once in a while we even take out the old sleigh and attend a real sporting event, although we always have to be careful not to bump into those pesky blimps.

Swapping sports jokes is a favorite pastime of ours, so naturally we think we've hit a grand slam with what you're about to read. This book has been a real team effort. We've tackled the job and, from our "pole" position, covered all the bases.

Wherever your holiday travels take you, we invite you to go the distance with Santa's Favorite Sports Jokes, the odds-on favorite for fan-tastic fun.

*Santa Claus*

# THE SPORTS FAN'S PRAYER

*Thank you for baseball which comes in the spring*
*And for all the great bouts we see in the ring.*
*Thank you for satellite dishes, big screen TV's and such*
*And for cheerleaders, thank you, thank you ever so much.*

*Thank you for race cars which rack up the laps*
*And for golf on TV so we can catch up on naps.*
*We thank you for colorful coaches with differing styles*
*And for hockey players with their picket-fence smiles.*

*Thank you for sports bars and nachos and all the good snacks*
*And for those comfy recliners which cradle our backs.*
*Thanks for Olympic athletes with confidence brimming*
*But you might want to re-think that synchronized swimming.*

*The Final Four, the Series and the great Super Bowl*
*Are all things that make it worth having a soul.*
*And since you've given us all these sports to enjoy*
*We thank you to forgive us for those we annoy.*

Have you heard about the collegiate football star who's been an undergraduate for eight years?

He can run and tackle with the best of them...but he can't pass.

❄ ❄ ❄

Q: What do you call a New Orleans Saint wearing a Super Bowl ring?

A: Thief

❄ ❄ ❄

Did you hear about the short music afficionado who tried out for the Olympics?

He's a compact disc thrower.

*Baseball is ninety percent mental. The other half is physical.*

—Yogi Berra

*My doctor told me that jogging could add years to my life. I think he was right. I feel ten years older already.*

—Milton Berle

A bush league baseball player is trying to impress the superstar in spring training. He brags, "Hey, I use a limo wherever I go."

The superstar responds, "Is that so? How long have you been a chauffeur?"

❄ ❄ ❄

Q: Why are boxers good at geometry?

A: Because they're used to circling in a squared ring

A lawyer was reading the will of a wealthy man to members of his family. As he neared the end of it, the lawyer read aloud, "And to my son Waldo, whom I promised to remember in my will even though he played golf all the time and never worked a day in his life...Hi there, Waldo!"

❄ ❄ ❄

A Boston marathoner suffered a sudden spell of dizziness so he stopped for a minute and rested his head between his legs.

Seeing this, a preppy Harvard student asked in very proper fashion, "Have you vertigo?"

The marathoner said, "Yes. Four more miles."

*He's the first guy to drive a $300,000 car with license plates he made himself.*

—Jay Leno, after Mike Tyson was released from prison and bought four Bentleys

*Tennis is like marrying for money. Love
has nothing to do with it.*

—Phyllis Diller

Muggsy and Buggsy had been together in Hell
for many, many years. Their eternal job was
to shovel coal into the fires side by side.

Suddenly, one day they felt cold air. The air got
colder and colder. Snow began to fall. The next
thing they knew, there was a blizzard. The snow
blanketed the ground and extinguished the fires.
Next, a gust of frigid wind froze over the entire
surface of Hell!

"What the heck is going on here?" Muggsy
wondered out loud.

Buggsy answered, "I don't know for sure, but
I have a hunch that the Bills just won the Super
Bowl."

A n avid football fan was hollerin' and hootin' all game long. He grew more and more hoarse as the pigskin contest went on until finally, in the fourth quarter, he whispered to the guy sitting next to him, "I think I've lost my voice."

The other guy replied, "Don't worry. You'll find it in my right ear."

*We lost every week. We lost to schools I never heard of. I think guys used to get together and invent a name just so they could play us. One year we lost to a school called 'We Want U.'"*

—Bill Cosby, on the pitiful pigskin team he played on at Temple University

*I don't think the coach likes me. He told*
*me to stand in front of the Zamboni.*

—Snoopy

A guy goes to confession. He says, "Father, forgive me, for I have sinned. I was skiing when I saw my boss on the same slope. He didn't recognize me because I was wearing my ski mask so I skied over to where he was, pushed him and roared with laughter as he rolled over and over down the hill."

"Why are you telling me this again?" asks the priest. "That's the fifth time you've confessed this transgression."

The guy answers, "I know. I just like talking about it."

**D**id you hear about the pitcher and his expectant wife?

They both suffered from complete exhaustion in the ninth.

❄ ❄ ❄

**A** gridiron star's friend says to him, "Hey, Buddy, I heard you got engaged."

"Nah, it's off," the football player says. "Just last night she said she'd be true to the end."

"So...what's wrong with that?"

"I'm the quarterback."

*It doesn't matter whether you win or lose until you lose.*

—Anonymous

*In football the object is to march into enemy territory and cross his goal. In baseball the object is to go home.*

—George Carlin, on the difference between the two sports

One Sunday morning, a big, brusque umpire asked his son to hop on his lap so he could read the kid the funny papers. The boy refused because the son never sits on the brutish umpire.

❄ ❄ ❄

Q: When was the first tennis match?
A: When Moses served in Pharoah's court

A nd then there was the fighter who couldn't find anything to drink. Someone beat him to the punch.

## HO-HO-HO!

S anta's a pretty good heavyweight in his own right. In fact, he's the boxing champ of the North Pole. Do you know why he always wears bells when he tips the scales before a fight?

He likes to jingle all the weigh.

*All pro athletes are bilingual. They speak English and profanity.*

—Gordie Howe

# *Punchlines*

**M**aybe you heard about the Mafioso type who dubbed himself "The Pugilistic Engineer." He made a career of fixing fights.

**T**hen there was the colorful fighter. He was black and blue all over.

**A** good fighter always considers the rights of others.

**T**he toughest thing about fighting is picking up your teeth with your boxing gloves on.

**T**he fight manager nicknamed his boxer "Laundry"...Seems he was always hanging over the ropes.

**F**ighters make money hand over fist.

**D**id you hear about the fighter who had the misfortune of breaking his nose in two places? He vowed never to go back to either of them.

A frustrated golfer, whose ball was lost in the rough, annoyedly asked his caddie, "Why must you constantly be looking at that pocket watch?"

The caddie responded, "Oh, it's not a pocket watch, sir. It's a compass."

❋ ❋ ❋

Q: What do you get when you cross a football player with someone who lives in a church bell tower?

A: The Halfback of Notre Dame

*It wasn't as easy as you think. It's hard to stay awake that long.*

—Whitworth College football coach Hugh Campbell, after defeating Whitman 70-30

*You know, when the World Cup is over all these people will go home. Which means the only people bouncing balls off their heads will be the Chicago Cubs outfielders.*

—Jay Leno

## HO-HO-HO!

What did the Notre Dame football coach write on his Christmas cards?

Irish you a Merry Christmas.

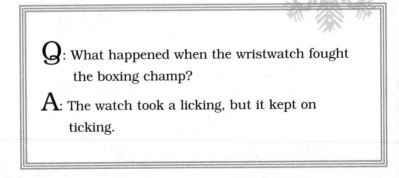

Q: What happened when the wristwatch fought the boxing champ?

A: The watch took a licking, but it kept on ticking.

S atan proposed a baseball game between Heaven and Hell. St. Peter smiled, "It wouldn't be fair. We have all the great ones...Mantle, Ruth, Gehrig and all the rest."

Satan responded, "Ah, but we have all the umpires."

❄ ❉ ❄

Q: What do old bowling balls become?

A: Marbles for elephants

*He didn't know anything about drugs.*

*He thought uppers were dentures.*

—Two time Heisman Trophy winner
Archie Griffin on Ohio State
coach Woody Hayes

*I'm waiting for the day we see the 'wave'*
*at the Metropolitan Opera.*

—Al Michaels

M illie: What has eight legs and an IQ of forty?

Tillie: Four guys watching a football game.

❄ ❄ ❄

A nd then there was the slumping pole vaulter.
His vaults weren't quite up to bar.

❄ ❄ ❄

Q: Why was the artist in the boxing ring?

A: Because the fight ended in a draw

A guy's at a basketball game seated in the middle of a row. He gets up to get a hot dog and soda. When he returns he says to the woman who's sitting at the end of the aisle, "Excuse me. Did I step on your foot when I went out?"

Expecting an apology, the woman answers, "Why yes, you did."

Instead the guy says, "Good...that means this is my row."

*I competed in the long jump, because it seemed to be the only event where afterward you didn't fall down and throw up.*

—Dave Barry

# SPORTS HOROSCOPE

**Aquarius (Jan 20-Feb 18) The Office Pool**
Born under the sign of the office pool, you can soon
expect to pick up a bundle at the track. Just be sure to
spread it around the rose bushes as soon as possible.

**Pisces (Feb 19-Mar 20) The Protective Cup**
The conjunction of Mars and Jupiter will bring you
the "Most Valuable Player" award after the big game.
Unfortunately, it'll be from your poker buddies.

**Aries (Mar 21-Apr 19) The Beer Belly**
All your friends consider you the biggest sports fan
they know. That's because when it comes to blowing a
lot of hot air around, you da' man!

**Taurus (Apr 20-May 20) The Armchair Quarterback**
The stars say you can expect to be on the cover of
*Sports Illustrated.* Someone will leave it on the bench
just before you sit down.

**Gemini (May 21-Jun 21) The Ref**
The transit of Neptune means that you're not all that
athletic. Most guys stay in shape by pumping iron.
Your idea of staying in shape is pumping gas.

**Cancer (Jun 22-Jul 22) The Jock**
Your softball skills will earn you much fame. You'll be
invited to Times Square next New Year's Eve for a
special honor...They'll want you to drop the ball.

**Leo (Jul 23-Aug 22) The Sports Bar**
You spend so much time watching baseball, you actually believe that the last words to the national anthem are "Play Ball!"

**Virgo (Aug 23-Sep 22) The Season Pass**
Your talents will lead you to develop a new workout program for sports fans—"Beer-oebics"—zip, lift, chug, crunch, zip, lift, chug, crunch...

**Libra (Sep 23-Oct 23) The Catcher's Mitt**
You possess the physique of a champion skier... going downhill fast.

**Scorpio (Oct 24-Nov 21) The Bench**
When it comes to football, you'll play in the Ivy League. After every game, you'll wind up attached to an I-V.

**Sagittarius (Nov 22-Dec 21) The Six Pack**
Soon, your appearance on the field will hearten and inspire the entire team...too bad it's the opposing team.

**Capricorn (Dec 22-Jan 19) The Groin Pull**
The stars portend that you will some day be the starting pitcher for the New York Yankees. Of course, that will only be when the regular water boy is late.

*I'm one of the few to ever throw a javelin*
*two hundred yards. Well, actually I only*
*threw it one hundred yards. The guy it hit*
*crawled the other hundred.*

—Jose Jimenez
(the alter ego of Bill Dana)

A couple of tourists from Greece were at a football game. At halftime one said to the other, "Do you have any idea what's going on here?"

The other replied, "No, it's all English to me."

❄ ❄ ❄

Then there was the crossword puzzle boxer. He came into the ring vertically and always left horizontally.

A guy goes to a psychiatrist and says, "Doc, I need help. I just can't seem to make decisions."

The doctor says, "Actually, that's not so unusual. Lots of people have a tough time making up their minds."

"Yeah, but I'm an umpire."

❄ ❄ ❄

Q: Why was Cinderella a lousy football player?

A: Because she had a pumpkin for a coach

*I'll shoot my age if I live to be 105.*

—Bob Hope, on golf

*There's a fine line between fishing and just standing on the shore looking like an idiot.*

—Steven Wright

Maybe you know that George Foreman's careers have been in boxing and preaching. That's why some people call him a pewgilist.

❄ ❄ ❄

Q: What do you get when you cross a groundhog and a basketball player?

A: Six more weeks of hoops

A cricket ambled into a sporting goods store in London. The store's owner, somewhat taken aback to see a cricket with an interest in sports, said, "Hey, we have a popular game that goes by your name!"

"You're kidding," said the cricket. "You have a game called Jiminy?"

❄ ❆ ❄

Q: What do you get when you cross an English bathroom with Kareem Abdul-Jabbar?

A: Loo Alcindor

*I still think neckties are designed to get in your soup.*

—Baseball Hall of Famer Ted Williams

*Kids should practice autographing
baseballs. This is a skill that's often
overlooked in Little League.*

—Tug McGraw

Maybe you heard about the wide receiver they call "Touchdown Tony." One touch and down he went.

❋ ❊ ❋

A cat is watching a tennis match. Another cat strolls by and says, "Why are you watching that. Cats don't like tennis."

"I know but my father's in the racket."

A snail bought a particularly impressive race car and decided to enter the Indianapolis 500. To give the car a distinctive look, the snail had a big letter S painted on the hood, sides and trunk before the big race. When the race began, the snail's car immediately took the lead, prompting one of the spectators to say, "Look at that S car go!"

*I've been an optimist since I was a kid. I can still remember the Christmas morning I ran down to my stocking and found it full of horse manure. I yelled, "Hey, I got a pony around here somewhere."*

—Former Michigan State football coach Duffy Daugherty

*Physical fitness is in. I recently had a
physical fit myself.*

—Steve Allen

The football player showed up with two water bottles, one full and one empty. A teammate asked him, "How come you have an empty bottle there?"

"Isn't it obvious?" he remarked. "That's in case I *don't* get thirsty."

❄ ❄ ❄

Did you hear about the marathoner who lost because of his socks?

They were guaranteed not to run.

The English teacher instructed the class to write a composition about the national pastime. Wiseacre Wally turned in his paper just a few moments later. It read, "Game postponed due to rain."

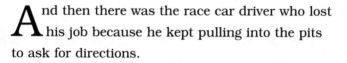

And then there was the race car driver who lost his job because he kept pulling into the pits to ask for directions.

*Anthropologists have discovered a 50-million-year-old human skull with three perfectly preserved teeth intact. They're not sure, but they think it may be the remains of the very first hockey player.*

—Jay Leno

*This will be the first time in the history*

*of the league (NBA) that the referee drops*

*the ball.*

—Broadcaster Dan Issel, on a
jump ball between 5'10"
Michael Adams and
5'3" Muggsy Bogues

A slick-fielding baseball player was walking by a burning building. A mother with a baby in her arms yelled to him from the third floor. The ballplayer told her to drop the baby. She let go, he caught the baby, then whirled and threw it to first base.

❋ ❋ ❋

Football centers make snap decisions.

The psychiatrist said to his patient, "You're finally cured. You no longer think you're Frank Gifford."

"That's terrific," the patient said. "Wait 'til I tell Kathie Lee the news!"

❄ ❄ ❄

"You really had him worried in the ninth round," said the trainer to his defeated and downtrodden fighter. "He thought he'd killed you."

*Now there's three things you can do in a baseball game: you can win or you can lose or it can rain.*

　　　　　—Casey Stengel

*Show me a boxing ring and I'll show you*
*a punch bowl.*

—Henny Youngman

Former baseball manager Casey Stengel, the "ol' perfessor" as he was affectionately known, found the proverbial genie in a lamp one day. After he rubbed the lamp, the genie appeared and said, "Casey, I have come to grant you one of three wishes. Which do you choose...infinite beauty, infinite wealth, or infinite wisdom?"

Casey pondered for a moment, then replied, "Infinite wisdom."

POOOOFF!! The genie disappeared and Casey uttered his first words of infinite wisdom.

"Darn! I should have taken the money."

# HO-HO-HO!

**Q**: What goes "Ho-Ho-Ho Swish?"

**A**: Santa sinking a jump shot

---

**M**oe: My watch says it's eight-ish.

Larry: That's funny...Mine says it's nine-ish.

Curly: Ten-ish, anyone?

---

*Last Christmas my father gave me a bat.*

*First time I tried to play with it, it flew away.*

—Rodney Dangerfield

*Nobody in the game of football should be
called a genius. A genius is somebody like
Norman Einstein.*

—Football commentator and former
quarterback Joe Theisman

"**B**asketball, basketball, basketball...that's all
you ever think of," complained the wife. "Why
I'll bet you don't even know the day we were
married."

"Of course I do, dear," said the husband. "It was
the night Wilt Chamberlain scored 100 points."

**Q**: What do Stefi Graf and a waitress have in
common?

**A**: They both know how to serve.

# *HO-HO-HO!*

Johnny: Mommy, I can't find my baseball mitt.

Mommy: Did you look in the car?

Johnny: Where in the car?

Mommy: The glove compartment.

---

How does Bobby Knight change a light bulb?

He yells and yells until the ref changes it for him.

---

*Your Holiness, I'm Joseph Medwick. I, too,*
*used to be a Cardinal.*

—"Ducky" Medwick, former St. Louis
      Cardinal, addressing the Pope

*What do you have when you've got an*
*agent buried up to his neck in the sand?*
*Not enough sand.*

—Orlando Magic general manager
Pat Williams

---

E gbert is at the doctor's for a physical. The doctor can't help but notice that his shins are covered with bruises and comments, "You must play either hockey or soccer."

Egbert says, "No, my wife and I are bridge players."

❄ ❖ ❄

A jockey got hurt when he fell off his horse. He was rushed to a nearby hospital. A few hours later one of his colleagues phoned the hospital and asked the nurse how his buddy was doing.

She said, "Well, you're a jockey so you should know. He's in stable condition."

There were just six seconds left on the clock of a tied pigskin contest. The quarterback threw a Hail Mary pass to the first-year wide receiver. He made a spectacular catch only to be hammered by the opposing cornerback. The ball fell loose and was picked up by a defender who ran the ball all the way for a game-ending touchdown. When the coach was asked about the heartbreaking defeat, he responded, "That's the way the rookie fumbles."

*Baseball players are smarter than football players. How many times do you see a baseball team penalized for too many men on the field?*

—Jim Bouton

*I ain't doing a damn thing, and I don't start until noon.*

—Ex-NFL coach Bum Phillips,
on his retirement

A teacher asked her students to list, in their opinions, the five greatest Americans. Little Johnny was taking longer than the others with his list.

"Have you finished yet, Johnny?" asked the teacher.

"Almost," responded Johnny, "but I'm having a tough time deciding on the point guard."

Q: When do bowling pins lie down?

A: When they are on strike

The manager strolls out to the mound to relieve his pitcher. The southpaw says, "C'mon coach. I struck this guy out the last time he was up."

The manager replies, "Yeah, but we're in the same inning."

❄ ❄ ❄

And then there was the horse that was so slow he won the next race.

*I went to a fight the other night and a hockey game broke out.*

—Rodney Dangerfield

*Prayer never seems to work for me on the golf course. I think this has something to do with my being a terrible putter.*

—Reverend Billy Graham

Clem is sitting in his Barcalounger reading the newspaper when he comes across an article about the Hollywood bombshell who married the not too bright fighter.

"I don't get it. The dumbest dorks get the most gorgeous girls," says Clem.

His wife answers, "Why, thank you. That's very kind of you, dear."

Doctor Dudley, toting his golf bag, was heading out of his dentist's office when his receptionist said, "Doctor, I have Mr. Arnold on the line. He has a toothache."

Dudley answered, "Tell him to call back tomorrow. I've got eighteen cavities to fill today."

Q: Where did they put the matador who joined the baseball club?

A: In the bullpen

*The most important rule of horseshoes is, first remove the horse.*

—Milton Berle

*My father-in-law and I have a great deal
in common. We both love football, golf,
and his daughter...not necessarily in
that order.*

—Lou Holtz

**49**ers quarterback Steve Young was poked in the eye during a pileup. He went to the sideline where the trainer recommended he put on an eye patch. Young felt it might hurt his peripheral vision on one side so he refused. Before he went back into the game his coach advised him to rely on the peeper that was okay as he said, "Remember, only the good eye, Young."

A nd then there was the boxing referee who had a former job at a space rocket launching site. Any time a fighter was knocked down he'd count, "Ten, nine, eight..."

\* \* \*

Q: What do you get if you cross a bowling lane with a famous heavyweight boxer?

A: Muhammad Alley

*Our similarities are different.*

—Dale Berra, on comparisons between him and his father, Yogi

# HO·HO·HO!

Three colleges are wooing a high school football star. The player shows up at Notre Dame where he notices a gold telephone on the athletic director's desk. He asks, "What's that phone for?"

"Oh, that," replies the athletic director. "That's the hot line to heaven."

"Gee, could I borrow it?" asks the football star.

"Sure, but it'll cost you 100 dollars a minute."

"Oh, that's too steep for me."

The player visits the University of Michigan next and sees a blue phone on the athletic director's desk.

"What's that blue telephone for?" the player asks the athletic director.

"That's our hot line to heaven."

The football star asks, "Can I make a call?"

"Yeah, but you'll have to reimburse us 100 dollars a minute."

"Oh, gee. I don't have that kind of money. Thanks anyway."

For the third leg of his college visits, the football player goes to North Pole University. There, he sees Santa in his office with a red phone at his desk.

"What's that red phone for, Santa?" asks the player.

"Ho ho ho! Why, that's our hot line to heaven."

"Mind if I borrow it?"

"Sure, but we have to keep our phone bills to a minimum so we can use all our resources for making the toys for all the boys and girls. I'm afraid I'll have to ask you to pay for it."

"And how much is that, Santa?"

"Fifteen cents a minute."

"Fifteen cents a minute to call heaven! Wow! How come it's so cheap?" asks the footballer.

Santa answers, "Because it's only a local call."

*I don't believe for a second weightlifting is a sport. They pick up a heavy thing and put it down again. To me, that's indecision.*

—Paula Poundstone

The diehard sports fan told his friend, "I've gotta cut down on hot dogs and beer."

"How come?"

"Because I'm starting to get a ballpark figure."

Did you hear about the football brute who wrote "TGIF" on his cleats? He wanted to be reminded that "Toes Go In First."

A golfing fanatic married a woman whose favorite pastime was attending auctions. Both husband and wife habitually talked in their sleep. One night the golfer yelled, "Fore."

His wife immediately countered, "Four fifty!"

❄ ❅ ❄

B aseball Player #1: How'd you make out with the owner's daughter?

Baseball Player #2: Horrible...no hits, no runs, no heiress.

*The only good (tennis) backhand I ever ran into was my mother's. She used it across my mouth.*

—Alan King

*I prefer rugby to soccer. When soccer
players start biting each other's ears off
again, maybe I'll like it better.*

—Elizabeth Taylor

"Doc, I need help," says Mort to the psychiatrist. "It may sound strange but I keep thinking that I'm a horse."

"I think I can cure you," the psychiatrist answers, "but it's going to take some time and it's going to be extremely expensive."

"Money's not a problem, Doc. I just won the Kentucky Derby."

Boss: What's the big idea of calling in sick yesterday?

Employee: I was sick.

Boss: You didn't look sick at the racetrack.

Employee: You should have seen me after the seventh race.

Then there was the ballplayer who had sinus trouble. No one wanted to sign him.

*Unlike in other sports, in tennis if you are getting killed you are expected to stay out there and continue to get killed.*

—Bill Cosby

The Pope arrived at the Pearly Gates where St. Peter took him to his apartment...a small, one-room unit. As the Pontiff was settling in, he looked out the window and saw a limousine pull up in front of a mansion across the heavenly street. A big, burly guy dressed to the nines got out of the limo and was escorted by a couple of female angels into the palatial home.

"Wow! Who is that?" asked the Pope.

"Oh, that's Big John McFarland," replied St. Peter. "He was a baseball umpire."

"A baseball umpire?" the Pope said. "My gosh, I was the head of the Roman Catholic Church and all I've got is this tiny room. What magnanimous thing must he have done to be granted with such rewards?"

"To tell you the truth," answered St. Peter, "we have a whole bunch of popes up here, but McFarland is the first umpire we've had in centuries."

**D**id you hear about the Japanese businessman who tried to import ice hockey but failed?

It was unfortunate that no one had a yen for it.

❄ ❉ ❄

**R**iley: Why is it that George always seems to win at cards but loses at the track?

Fenster: That's because they won't let him shuffle the horses.

*I was 6'1" when I started fighting, but with all the uppercuts I'm up to 6'5".*

—The "Bayonne Bleeder," former heavyweight boxer Chuck Wepner

# Off the Wall
*Humorous Graffiti from Lavatories of the Land*

ATHLETE'S FOOT COMES FROM ATHLETE'S FEAT

OLD BOWLING BALLS WIND UP IN THE GUTTER

YOU CAN'T PLAY TENNIS
WITHOUT RAISING A RACKET

BASKETBALL PLAYERS TELL TALL TALES

A TIMEKEEPER IS A CLOCK-EYED MAN

OLD QUARTERBACKS NEVER DIE...
THEY JUST PASS AWAY

TENNIS PLAYERS HAVE A LOT OF FAULTS

SIAMESE TWINS LOVE DOUBLEHEADERS

BOXERS LOOK OUT FOR THE RIGHTS OF OTHERS

The long-winded baseball manager was on the hot stove banquet circuit. After a particularly lengthy speech he commented, "I'm sorry that I may have talked beyond the allotted time. I looked for a clock, but this room doesn't seem to have one."

A heckler from the back yelled out, "You didn't see the *calendar* by the door?"

*The reason women don't play football is because eleven of them would never wear the same outfit in public.*

—Phyllis Diller

*We're experiencing audio difficulties.*

—New York Mets
broadcaster Ralph Kiner

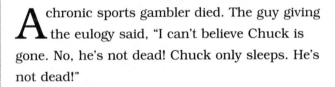

A chronic sports gambler died. The guy giving the eulogy said, "I can't believe Chuck is gone. No, he's not dead! Chuck only sleeps. He's not dead!"

With that, another gambler piped up, "I got a hundred bucks that says he's dead!"

❄ ❆ ❄

Q: How does Michael Jordan change a light bulb?

A: He fakes it out of its socket.

A guy from San Francisco, a guy from Detroit and a guy from Boston are granted a talk with God. They're each allowed one question. The guy from San Francisco inquires, "Will there ever be a time when we don't have to worry about earthquakes?"

God responds, "Yes, but not in your lifetime."

Then the guy from Detroit asks, "God, will there ever be a time when our city has no crime?"

Again God replies, "Yes, but not in your lifetime."

Finally, the guy from Boston asks, "God, will the Red Sox ever win the World Series?"

God answers, "Yes, but not in *my* lifetime!"

*A hard rubber disk that hockey players strike when they can't hit one another.*

—Columnist Jimmy Cannon's definition of a puck

*A horseshoe can't bring good luck because every horse in the race carries four.*

—Red Smith

Q: What do you get when you cross a hen with a bookmaker?

A: A chicken that lays odds

※ ❖ ※

Then there was the journeyman fighter who was everyone's punching bag. He was so bad the crowd always knew the result of his fight ten seconds before he did.

A little kid tells his mother that his father took him to the zoo. His mother says, "You've got to be kidding. There's no way he'd ever take you to the zoo."

The kid says, "He did...and one of the horses paid fifty dollars."

❄ ❄ ❄

Game Warden: Hey Buddy! What are you doing fishing here? Didn't you see the sign?

Fisherman: Sure...It says "Fine for Fishing."

*One of the nice things about the (golf)*
*Senior Tour is that we can take a cart and*
*cooler. If your game is not going well, you*
*can always have a picnic.*

—Lee Trevino

A doctor, an architect and a baseball player arrive at the Pearly Gates. St. Peter greets them and says, "We're just about filled to capacity. There's only room for one of you so it'll have to be the one whose profession is mentioned first in the Bible."

The doctor immediately pipes up, "That has to be me. God took a rib from Adam to make Eve. There's no doubt a medical procedure was necessary."

"Hold it," says the architect. "Adam and Eve came after the earth was created. Obviously, an architect came up with the blueprints to create the world as we know it."

The baseball player cries out, "Wait just a second! St. Peter...you said the one to get into heaven would be the guy whose job was mentioned first in the Bible, right?"

St. Peter replies, "Yes. And you think your profession is the one?"

"No doubt about it," grins the ballplayer. "Open up the Bible and there it is...the very first words, 'In the big inning...'"

A couple of guys are sitting at the bar having a conversation when one of them says, "Florida State! The only people that go to Florida State are football players and ugly women."

With that, the other guy, a big bruiser, gets up and says, "Hey! My wife went to Florida State!"

The first guy thinks quickly and says, "Oh, really? What position did she play?"

*The thing I like about football is that you don't have to take a shower before you go to work.*

—Former Chicago Bears
center Jay Hilgenberg

*As a nation we are dedicated to keeping physically fit...and parking as close to the stadium as possible.*

—Bill Vaughn

**Q**: What's a football player with good intuition called?

**A**: A hunchback

**D**id you hear about the businessman who opened a combination bowling lane/basketball court?

He named it Alley Hoop.

he gambler was so ecstatic at having bet on a 100 to one longshot which won the race that he rushed over to the winner's circle and planted a big kiss on the horse's face. The snooty owner of the horse frowned upon the gambler and said, "I say, Security...remove this man from the premises. How dare you do that to my horse!"

The gambler retorted, "I'm terribly sorry, my jolly good fellow. I thought it was your wife!"

*Skiing is the only sport where you spend an arm and a leg to break an arm and a leg.*

—Anonymous

*The good Lord was good to me. He gave
me a strong body, a good right arm, and a
weak mind.*

—Hall of Fame pitcher Dizzy Dean

The challenger was getting clobbered by the heavyweight champ. After the first round he stumbled back to his corner where his trainer said, "Let him hit you with left hooks in the second. Your face is crooked."

❄ ❄ ❄

Q: Why is it so difficult to drive a golf ball?

A: Because it doesn't have a steering wheel

Riley says to his psychiatrist, "I'm obsessed with baseball, Doc. It's taken over my life. I eat, drink and think baseball. I even sleep baseball. I dream about it every night. The second I close my eyes I'm running the base paths, fielding a grounder or chasing a fly ball. I wake up more tired than before I went to bed. What can I do, Doc?"

The psychiatrist replies, "The first thing you have to do is to make a conscious effort not to think about the game. For example, when you close your eyes make believe you're watching the lottery results on TV and—wow!—you just won a million dollars!"

"What are you, nuts, Doc?" cries Riley. "I'll miss my turn at bat!"

*If I had to choose between my wife and my putter, well, I'd miss her.*

—Gary Player

*We were so poor, every Christmas Eve my old man would go outside and shoot his gun, then come in and tell us kids that Santa Claus had committed suicide.*

—Boxer Jake LaMotta

Then there was the football matchup between two last place teams. It was called the Game of the Weak.

❄ ❄ ❄

Q: Why did they stop selling beer at the doubleheader?

A: Because the home team lost the opener

Q: What's the only creature that can take thousands of people for a ride at the same time?

A: A racehorse

❄ ❅ ❄

It was Sunday morning and the clergyman should have been at church instead of the bowling alley. He rolled a 300 for his third game, looked up at the heavens and cried, "A perfect game and I can't tell anybody!"

*I want to gain fifteen hundred or two thousand yards, whichever comes first.*

—Running back George Rogers

*I like everything about hockey except the game.*

—Glenn Hall

A fighter was in the ring with Siamese twins. After the bout he returned home and his wife asked, "Did you win?"

He answered, "Yes and no."

❋ ❋ ❋

Q: What do you get when you cross a fighter with a telephone?

A: A boxing ring

A guy with a little dog under his arm walks into a French Quarter bar in New Orleans one Sunday afternoon. He sits on a stool and places the dog on a stool beside him. A football game is on the television at the bar.

The guy orders a beer and asks the bartender, "What's the score of the Saints game? My dog and I are Saints fans."

The bartender says, "The Packers are leading thirteen to nuthin'."

No sooner did the bartender say that than the Saints returned a kickoff for a touchdown. The dog then stood up on the bar stool and started doing somersaults.

"Wow! That's really something," says the bartender.

"Oh, he does that every time the Saints score a touchdown," declares the dog's owner.

"If he does that for a touchdown, what does he do when the Saints win?"

The guy replies, "I wouldn't know. I've only had him for three years."

*The invention of basketball was not an accident. It was developed to meet a need. Those boys simply would not play Drop the Handkerchief.*

—Basketball's inventor,
Dr. James Naismith

The runner rounded third and headed for the plate as the leftfielder uncorked a beautiful throw home. The ball and the sliding runner arrived at the plate at the same time.

"You're out!" bellowed the umpire.

"No, I'm not out!" insisted the runner.

"You're not?" said the umpire. "I'll tell you what. We'll just see what it says in tomorrow's paper."

Q: How are the Denver Nuggets like fine wine?

A: Both are used to being in the cellar.

✳ ✣ ✳

Then there was the dentist who complimented the hockey player on his nice, even teeth: one, three, five, seven and nine were missing.

*If we did get a divorce, the only way he would know it is if they announced it on "Wide World of Sports."*

—Dr. Joyce Brothers,
on her armchair
quarterback husband

*Having children is like having a bowling alley installed in your brain.*

—Martin Mull

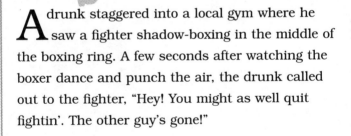

A drunk staggered into a local gym where he saw a fighter shadow-boxing in the middle of the boxing ring. A few seconds after watching the boxer dance and punch the air, the drunk called out to the fighter, "Hey! You might as well quit fightin'. The other guy's gone!"

❄ ❄ ❄

Q: How does Brett Favre change a light bulb?
A: He passes the job to a receiver.

A horse shows up at an open tryout for the New York Yankees. The manager doesn't take the horse too seriously, but nonetheless, allows him to take some swings in the batting cage. Much to his surprise, the horse is an unbelievable power hitter and after clubbing ten homers in a row the Yankees decide to sign him up.

That night, the horse is sitting on the bench. In the bottom of the ninth, with two men out and the Yankees trailing 2-1, the horse is called on to pinch-hit. He steps up to the plate, cracks the first pitch off the centerfield wall and just stands there.

Everyone in the dugout is standing and yelling, "Run! Run!"

The horse say, "Run! Hrrmmmmph! If I could run, I'd be at Aqueduct."

*All the lies about him are true.*

—Joe Dugan, on his former teammate Babe Ruth

*I believe in rules. Sure I do. If there weren't any rules, how could you break them?*

—Leo Durocher

The turtles and skunks decide to have a soccer match. The turtle's team is slow as molasses while the skunk's team just plain stinks. The game is scoreless with just seconds to go when, suddenly, a centipede—picked up as a ringer by the skunks—rushes onto the field, gets a pass, dribbles the ball, shoots and scores as the shell-shocked turtles watch the game go by the boards.

Afterwards, the coach of the skunks asks the centipede, "Where have you been all game?"

The centipede answers, "I was stringing up my cleats."

Then there was the Russian tennis player who's game was great at the nyet.

❋ ❋ ❋

Q: How many college basketball players does it take to screw in a light bulb?

A: One...but he gets three credits for it.

*There exists an inverse correlation between the size of a ball and the quality of writing about the sport in which the ball is used. There are superb books about golf, very good books about baseball, not very many good books about football, very few good books about basketball, and there are no good books on beachballs.*

—George Plimpton

*You never know with these psychosomatic*

*injuries. You have to take your time with them.*

—Baseball Hall of Famer
Jim Palmer

A Jewish football player received a scholarship to Notre Dame. When there was a semester break, he flew home. His rabbi bumped into him at the airport. Aware that the player was a member of the Fighting Irish football team the rabbi said, "Tell me, son. They haven't converted you to their ways, have they?"

The football star answered, "Why, no...absolutely not, Father!"

Three guys desperately want to get into the Olympic stadium but the Games are sold out so they decide to pose as athletes. The first guy picks up a long piece of pipe, walks up to the athletes' entrance and says to the guard, "I'm a pole vaulter."

The guard lets him in.

The second guy appears with a manhole cover and says, "Discus thrower."

He's also allowed in.

The third guy shows up with some barbed wire and says, "Fencing."

*The serve was invented so the net could play.*

—Bill Cosby

*I'm making fifty pigs in a blanket for twenty pigs in the living room.*

—Roseanne, on preparing
a Super Bowl party

A fighter's taking a licking and after round one he goes back to the corner where his trainer advises him, "When you get knocked down, stay down until eight."

The fighter says, "Okay...what time is it now?"

**Q**: What part of the fish do most anglers bring home?

**A**: The tale

A baseball player died and went to Heaven. Once up there, he was able to look down to Hell where he saw the most spectacular stadium with a capacity crowd, players on the field and a batter at the plate. "Boy, St. Peter," the ballplayer said. "It looks like a game is just about to start. You call that Hell? I'd love to be playing there."

"That's just it," smiled St. Peter. "So would they, but they don't have a ball."

*Since we're a one-man team, John Elway has a curfew. The rest can do what they want.*

—Former Broncos coach
Dan Reeves

*Never wash your ball on the tee of a*

*water hazard.*

—Anonymous

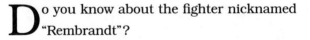

D o you know about the fighter nicknamed "Rembrandt"?

His face was always on the canvas.

❋ ❋ ❋

H ow about the fighter nicknamed "Submarine Sal"?

Seems he was always taking a dive.

An angry homeowner says to a kid, "Have you seen who broke my window?"

The kid replies, "No but have you seen my baseball?"

Did you hear about the wide receiver named Cinderella?

Seems he kept missing the ball.

*I went fishing with a dotted line. I caught every other fish.*

—Steven Wright

*On the day of the race, a lot of people*
*want you to sign something just before*
*you get in the car so that they can say*
*they got your last autograph.*

—A.J. Foyt

## HO-HO-HO!

**Q**: How do Santa's reindeer start a race?
**A**: Someone says, "Ready, set...*doe*!"

---

A golfer complained to his caddy, "You're such a wiseguy. When we get back to the clubhouse I'm gonna make sure the pro fires you."

The caddy shot back, "Fine, because by the time we get back I'll be old enough to get a regular job."

A college basketball coach scouted a high school player with unbelievable talent. The kid was 7'1" and had great offensive and defensive skills. Unfortunately, his academic skills didn't match. The coach begged the academic dean to admit the kid to the school. Finally, the dean agreed to let the kid in if he could answer three math questions.

The kid was brought in to the dean's office where he was asked the first question.

"What's two and two?" asked the dean.

The kid pondered for a few painful moments and finally replied, "Four."

"How much is four and four?"

The kid thought even longer this time before saying, "Eight."

"And now, for your final question, how much is eight and eight?"

The kid paused and paused and paused and then blurted out, "Sixteen."

With that, the coach begged to the dean, "Please! Please! Give him one more chance!"

*If it wasn't for golf, I'd probably be a caddie today.*

—George Archer

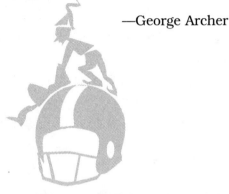

Ruppert Nerdock, the newspaper magnate, spent oodles of money to buy a racehorse. The noted trainer Willie Shumaker offered to race his horse against Nerdock's. The night of the match race, the track was filled and sportswriters from all of Nerdock's newspapers were there. Unfortunately for Nerdock, his horse didn't live up to its billing and was beaten by nine lengths. The next day, the sports page headline on all of Nerdock's newspapers read: *NERDOCK'S HORSE FINISHES SECOND, SHUMAKER'S HORSE NEXT-TO-LAST.*

**Q**: How are a losing pro football team and an atheist alike?

**A**: Neither has a prayer on Sundays.

✳ ✤ ✳

**K**nock-knock.

Who's there?

Joe Namath.

Joe Namath who?

Joe Namath not on the door. That's why I knocked.

*If you drink, don't drive. Don't even putt.*

—Dean Martin

*I occasionally get birthday cards from
fans. But it's often the same message:
They hope it's my last.*

—Former National League
umpire Al Forman

## HO-HO-HO!

This sign was actually spotted outside an Illinois
health club:

MERRY FITNESS & HAPPY NEW REAR!

---

The fix was in. One crooked fight manager says
to the other, "Your guy will flatten mine at the
end of the first round. Okay?"

"Make it the fifth. After all, the people did come
to see a fight."

The doctor teaching a medical course at the college left the classroom briefly. The phone rang and one of the students answered it.

It was the school's football coach who said, "Doc, one of my players got hurt. He broke his arm in the second quarter."

The medical student said, "Uh huh. And just what part of the arm is that?"

*A sportsman is a man who, every now and then, simply has to get out and kill something. Not that he's cruel. He wouldn't hurt a fly. It's not big enough.*

—Stephen Leacock

# Santa's Top Ten Yogi-isms

That master of malaprops and baseball Hall of Famer, Yogi Berra, is one of Santa's all-time favorites. Here Santa presents his personal top ten quotes from Yogi.

1.  "When you come to the fork in the road, take it."

2.  "Ninety per cent of the game is half mental."

3.  "A nickel ain't worth a dime anymore."

4.  On the benefits of Little League: "It keeps the kids out of the house."

5.  "If people don't want to come to the ball park, how are you gonna stop them?"

6.  On refusing to buy new luggage: "You only use it for traveling."

7. "Nobody goes to that restaurant anymore. It's too crowded."

8. When asked for the correct time: "Do you mean now?"

9. Talking about the variety of sweaters he has: "The only color I don't have is navy brown."

10. "I really didn't say everything I said."

*One player was lost because he broke his nose. How do you go about getting a nose in condition for football?*

—Texas football coach Darrell Royal,
when asked if the season's abnormal
number of Longhorn injuries resulted
from poor physical conditioning

*Boxing is like ballet, except that there's no music, no choreography, and the dancers hit each other.*

—Anonymous

Two old geezers were out on the links. One of them was on the fairway while the other was searching in the rough. The foursome behind them was growing impatient. Finally, one of the four yelled to the old-timer on the fairway, "Hey, why don't you help your friend find his ball?"

The old guy shouted back, "He's got his ball. He's looking for his club."

S ign seen in tennis pro shop: *Sale on Balls. First Come, First Serve.*

❄ ❄ ❄

O ne racehorse bumps into another racehorse in the paddock. The first one says to the second, "Gee, your pace is familiar, but I don't remember your mane."

*Basketball develops individuality, initiative, and leadership. Now get out there and do exactly what I tell you to do.*

—Former coach turned broadcaster Dick Vitale

*All right, everyone line up alphabetically according to your height.*

—Casey Stengel

*HO-HO-HO!*

**Q**: What does a fisherman mail to his friends in December?

**A**: Christmas cods

---

**M**rs. Jones was giving her third-grade class a geography lesson. "Can anyone tell me where Baltimore is?" she asked the class.

Little Johnny raised his hand.

"Yes, Johnny."

"Baltimore is at Cleveland today."

A boxer arrived in New York with some time to kill before his fight at Madison Square Garden. He stopped in at a bar across the street from the Garden and hoisted a few too many. He staggered out of the bar and fell down the steps of the subway entrance next to Penn Station. Not realizing where he was, he wandered around for a while before managing to crawl back up the stairs and onto the street. He bumped into another boxer who was on the fight card. The other fighter noticed the disheveled and glazed look on the drunken boxer and said, "Where the heck have you been?"

The drunken boxer shook his head and responded, "I think I was down in some guy's basement and—wow!—has he got a set of trains!"

*A race track is a place where windows clean people.*

—Danny Thomas

*Statistics always remind me of the fellow
who drowned in a river whose average
depth was only three feet.*

—Woody Hayes

Two lions are talking. One says to the other,
"Boy, I'm so proud of my two kids."

The second lion says, "Oh yeah...what do they
do?"

"One plays on an NFL team and the other's in
the movies."

❄ ❄ ❄

Q: How do you make a slow horse fast?

A: Don't feed him.

Then there was the Cleveland baseball player who refused to sign his contract. He was a wouldn't Indian.

❄ ❄ ❄

A golfer was carefully lining up his putt when a ball whizzed by his ear, narrowly missing his head. After he putted out, a duffer came running up to him and apologized.

"I'm sorry," he said. "I would have yelled 'Fore!' but I didn't want to ruin your putt."

*Watching an Americas Cup race is like watching grass grow.*

—Ring Lardner

A guy desperately wants to go to the Super Bowl so he goes to a scalper but can get only one ticket. He pays top dollar for a seat in the nosebleed section, the second to last row of the upper deck. As the game begins, the guy's watching through his binoculars. He notices that there's an empty seat in the very first row, right on the fifty yard line. As the second quarter is about to end, he looks down and sees that the fifty yard line seat is still empty. At halftime, he makes his way down to the empty seat and asks the guy who's sitting in the next seat, "Is this taken?"

The guy replies, "No."

"Would you mind if I sit here?"

The other guy says, "Not at all. Go right ahead."

"I wonder why someone with a front row, fifty yard line seat wouldn't show up at the Super Bowl," says the first guy.

The second guy says, "Actually, my wife and I have come to every Super Bowl since 1967, but she passed away."

"Oh, gee, I'm sorry to hear that," says the first guy. "But couldn't you get a friend or relative to come to the game?"

"They're all at the funeral."

Then there was the 7'2" basketball star who got his height from his parents. They were each 3'7".

✳ ✳ ✳

Maybe you've heard about the lousy fighter who was on the mat so often he wore out his welcome.

✳ ✳ ✳

**Q**: What do a musical conductor and a baseball statistician have in common?

**A**: They both know the score.

*They can make two hundred fifty bats out of one good tree. How's that for a statistic, baseball fans?*

—Andy Rooney

*The perils of duck hunting are great,*

*especially for the duck.*

—Walter Cronkite

# HO-HO-HO!

Did you hear the one about how Santa and Mrs. Claus got together?

For their third date, Santa took her to see a North Pole U football game.

While watching a tremendously talented freshman make one spectacular play after another, Santa excitedly said, "Next year, I expect him to be our best man."

To which she replied, "Oh Santa, this is so sudden!"

T he restaurant hostess said to the manager of the establishment, "There's a baseball umpire on the phone who wants to make dinner reservations for himself and three friends."

The manager said, "Hang up the phone. It's gotta be a crank call. There's no such thing as a baseball ump with three friends."

❋ ❋ ❋

Q: What do you call the NFL's out-of-control Baltimore offensive lineman?

A: A Raven lunatic

*Do you realize that's almost seven million dollars per tooth?*

—"Tonight Show" host Jay Leno, on hockey superstar Mario Lemieux' seven-year $42 million dollar contract

*I went through life as a player to be named later.*

—Joe Garagiola

Son: Hey, Dad! I won the broad jump at the track meet!

Father: That's great, but I thought you entered the discus throw.

Son: That's right...but as I was about to throw, I backed into a javelin.

❄ ❄ ❄

Q: What do you get when you cross a computer nerd with an Olympic athlete?

A: A floppy disk-us thrower

The army unit's boxing team needed one more fighter to fill out all the weight classes so they enlisted a soldier who'd never been in a fight in his life. The night of his first fight he was scared to death. After the fight, he came back to his barracks all beaten up...two black eyes and a bloody face beaten to the pulp.

"You look horrible," said his bunkmate.

"That's not the worst of it," said the soldier. "I gotta fight again tomorrow night. I won!"

*The trouble with the officials is they just don't care who wins.*

—Centenary College basketball
coach Tom Canterbury

"I can't believe my rotten luck," moaned Mulligan. "I haven't had a winning horse in more than two months."

"Hey, maybe you should try out my system," said Hoolihan. "It's worked pretty well for me lately."

"What system is that?" asked Mulligan.

"Well," answered Hoolihan, "it's pretty simple. Every day that I plan on going to the track, that morning I go to church and pray for ten minutes. I've had at least two winners a day since I've been doing that."

Mulligan was ready to try anything so, sure enough, the next morning he went to church and prayed for half an hour. Then it was off to the racetrack. At the end of the day, he ran into Hoolihan.

"That system of yours is patooie!" he complained to Hoolihan. "I went to church this morning, prayed three times as long as you do and didn't have a single winner all afternoon."

"Where did you go to church?" asked Hoolihan.

"To the one on Peach Street," said Mulligan.

"You idiot!" exclaimed Hoolihan. "That church is for trotters."

Then there was the pro football bruiser who was offered seven figures to pen his autobiography. A year later, he turned in the story of his Jeep.

※ ❋ ※

Did you hear about the dentist who was an avid baseball fan? During the day he yanked at roots and at night he did just the opposite.

*If God didn't want man to hunt, he wouldn't have given us plaid shirts.*

—Johnny Carson

*The Rose Bowl is the only bowl that I*
*have ever seen that I didn't have to clean.*

—Erma Bombeck

It's the state prison's championship game. There are two outs in the bottom of the ninth inning. The home team is down by one and the bases are loaded. The catcher walks out to the mound and says to the pitcher, "Take your time. You've got twenty years."

❄ ❄ ❄

**Q**: What happens if you hit a green golf ball into the Red Sea?

**A**: It gets wet.

B ubba and Butch, swift on the field but not so swift upstairs, have been recruited by a college for a scholarship, but first they have to take an admission exam. The football coach is ga-ga over these guys so he makes arrangements for a very easy test. The two players show up in a classroom all by themselves. Posted on the blackboard is their one-question exam: *Complete this sentence: Old MacDonald had a _____?*

Bubba writes down the answer immediately but Butch is perplexed. Finally, he leans over and asks, "Do you know the answer?"

Bubba answers, "Of course. Any idiot knows that."

"What is it, then?" asks Butch.

Bubba replies condescendingly, "It's 'farm,' you nitwit."

Butch then asks, "How do you spell it?"

Bubba responds, "E-I-E-I-O."

*They wanted an arm and a leg.*

—Former tennis star Martina
Navratilova, on why she never insured
her left arm with Lloyds of London

There was a very old fighter who had trouble
sleeping. His doctor advised him, "Just lie
down, relax and start counting to 100."

A week later the guy came back to the doctor
and said, "It's no use. I keep getting up at the
count of nine."

**Q**: What did the golfing caterpillar become
when he grew up?

**A**: A putter-fly

**T**wo Chicagoans are talking. "I was in the middle of the jungle once, armed with nothing but a pen when, all of a sudden, a lion approached and stared me down," said one.

"My gosh, what did you do?" asked the second.

"I grabbed my pen," said the first guy, "and quickly wrote on my arm 'the Cubs will win the World Series this year.'"

"How did that save you?"

"Simple...not even the king of the jungle would swallow that."

*I never cease to amaze myself. I say this humbly.*

—Don King

*Part of the charm of basketball is that it's
a simple game to understand. Players
race up and down a fairly small area
indoors and stuff the ball into a ring with
Madonna's dress hanging on it.*

—Dan Jenkins

Maybe you've heard about the jockey who was a tremendous overeater. He kept putting a la carte before the horse.

❄ ❅ ❄

Did you hear about the giant basketball player who became a prizefighter? He developed a cauliflower navel.

# HO·HO·HO!

Joe Jock, the college football player, showed up at the post office a few days before Christmas to mail a present to his mother.

The harried clerk took the package, weighed it and said, "I'm sorry...it's too heavy. You'll have to put more stamps on it."

"Gee," replied Joe Jock, "and people say *I'm* dumb. That'll only make it heavier!"

*They talk about the economy this year. Hey, my hairline is in recession, my waistline is in inflation. All together, I'm in a depression.*

—University of Utah basketball coach Rick Majerus

# *Q & A*

**Q**: How many sportscasters does it take to change a light bulb?

**A**: Two...one to change it and one to do color

**Q**: What happened to the two silkworms who had a match race?

**A**: They wound up in a tie.

**Q**: What's the difference between an umpire and a pickpocket?

**A**: An umpire watches steals...

**Q**: If a basketball team was running after a baseball team, what time would it be?

**A**: Five after nine

**Q**: What do you get when you cross a comedic actress with a hockey player?

**A**: Goalie Hawn

**M**ike says to his wife, Lynn, "I'm never playing golf with Kirk again. He claimed he found his lost ball two feet away from the green. What a cheat!"

"Well, isn't that possible?" asks Lynn.

"Not if I've got the ball in my pocket!"

*Well, if it's undisputed what's all the*

*fighting about?*

—George Carlin, on the heavyweight boxing title

Beethoven's Ninth Symphony was being performed at the famed Carnegie Hall. During intermission, the conductor becomes frantic when he realizes the last few pages of his sheet music are missing. After telling his assistant this, the trusted aide remembers that the missing pages were accidentally locked in the dressing room. He assures the conductor that they'll be on his music stand in time for when they are needed.

"I would hope so," growls the conductor. "And while you're at it, keep an eye on the bass players. They've been drinking ever since the intermission started."

The conductor then goes about his business while the assistant makes sure the bass players down a few cups of coffee before they return to their orchestra seats.

As the curtain rises for the remainder of the symphony, the assistant rushes to find a security guard who can open the dressing room. He finds one and hurries him down to the locked room.

"What's all the fuss about?" asks the security guard.

The assistant replies, "It's the bottom of the ninth, the score is tied, and the bassists are loaded!"

Quarterback: I passed your house this morning.

Tight end: Wow! What an arm!

❄ ✳ ❄

Q: What goes *gnip-gnop, gnip-gnop, gnip-gnop?*

A: A ping-pong ball bouncing backwards

*Whenever I play with him, I usually try to make it a foursome—the president, myself, a paramedic and a faith healer.*

—Bob Hope, on playing golf
with Gerald Ford

*There weren't many alleys that would let me come back. I have an overhand delivery.*

—John Wayne, on bowling

Myron: Hey, I heard you got a full-time 9-5 position at the racetrack! How do you like it?

Byron: The job's crummy but you can't beat the odds!

❄ ❄ ❄

The fighter staggered to his corner and asked his trainer, "What round is this?"

His trainer replied, "When the bell rings, it'll be the first."

$D$id you hear that because of U.S. Olympic Gold Medal skier Picabo Street's donations to a local Denver hospital, they're thinking about naming a new wing after her? It's going to be called 'Picabo, I.C.U.'

❄ ✳ ❄

$Q$: What do you get when a tiny, green, round vegetable picks a fight with a boxer?

$A$: A black-eyed pea

*I don't like to watch golf on television.*

*I can't stand whispering.*

—David Brenner

M ilt Famie was one of the top pitchers to have ever played for the Brewers. His only problem was his tolerance for alcohol. Famie could not hold the hard stuff so his teammates, coaches and friends always made sure he steered clear of it.

It was the night before a World Series game against the Cardinals (who knew that Famie would be pitching against them the next afternoon). A few of the Cardinals schemed a way to get Famie out of his hotel room and into the tavern next door by pretending to be movie producers who wanted to do a film on the hurler's life.

Famie had more than one too many beers at the tavern and, sure enough, the next day he couldn't find the plate. He walked the first six batters he faced before his manager mercifully removed him from the game. The two runs he gave up cost the Brewers the game as the Cardinals won, 2-1.

During the postgame press conference, Whitey Herzog, the Cardinals manager, was asked why he thought that the Brewers pitcher was so wild. Herzog, aware of his players prank, slyly remarked, "It's the beer that made Milt Famie walk us."

A not too bright boxer pleaded with his manager. "Listen to me. I'm in great shape. I been trainin' for eight months. My eatin' and drinkin' habits are great. I been goin' ta bed early and gettin' a good night's sleep every night. I'm tellin' ya, I've trained and trained and trained. Please, please...ya gotta let me fight Lefty Looie."

His manager responded, "If I told you once, I told you a million times...you *are* Lefty Looie!"

❄ ❄ ❄

Waiter:  And what would you like for dinner, sir?

Bowler:  Spare ribs

*If Casey Stengel were alive today, he'd be spinning in his grave.*

—Ralph Kiner

*If a woman has to choose between catching a fly ball and saving an infant's life, she will choose to save the infant's life without even considering if there are men on base.*

—Dave Barry

A turkey tries out for a baseball team. He's a natural...great power hitter, a terrific fielder and a speed demon on the base paths. The club's owner tells him, "Congratulations. You've made the team. We'll draw up a contract."

The turkey says, "I just want one clause in it... that we play through November."

# HO-HO-HO's from Henny

Santa's silly sidekick, the self-professed North Pole king of corn, Henny Elfman.

1. If athletes get athlete's foot, what do astronauts get?

2. What's Santa's favorite college football team?

3. What kind of animal lives at the North Pole and is good at strikes and spares?

4. Why aren't any of Santa's elves in the NBA?

5. How do Santa's reindeer get themselves in shape for their Christmas Eve journey?

Answers:
1. Missile-toe
2. Ida-ho-ho-ho
3. A bowler bear
4. They just don't measure up.
5. By doing ice-ometrics

*I have a lifetime contract. That means I
can't be fired during the third quarter if
we're ahead and moving the ball.*

—Lou Holtz

Football widow #1: You know, I think my husband really does love me, after all.

Football widow #2: What makes you say that?

Football widow #1: The other day he was watching football so I decided to change a light bulb myself. I got up on the ladder, promptly fell off and broke my leg.

Football widow #2: Why on earth would you think that means he loves you?

Football widow #1: He didn't wait till halftime to call the doctor.

A couch potato fell asleep watching *Monday Night Football*. His wife went to bed figuring he'd join her later. The next morning, to her surprise, she finds him still asleep on the couch. She nudges him and says, "Honey, get up. It's ten to nine."

He asks, "Who's winning?"

*No, I clean giraffe ears.*

—Elvin Hayes, former Washington Bullets (now Wizards) forward, when asked if he played basketball

A guy walks into a bar and does a double take when he sees a horse serving the drinks.

"What the heck is this?" the guy demands.

The horse responds, "Look, mister. I've been having a rough go of it lately. A few years ago I won the Kentucky Derby. It was all downhill from there. My filly left me for some other stud. I had problems with my feet so they retired me. This was the only job available to me."

The guy was flabbergasted...a genuine Mr. Ed!

He asks the horse if the owner is around. The horse points to the kitchen. The guy goes into the kitchen and says to the bar owner, "I'd love to buy your horse."

The owner says, "A hundred bucks and he's yours. That horse is the worst bartender I've ever seen."

The guy says, "A hundred bucks?...Sold!"

The owner says, "Before we shake on it, I've gotta come clean with you. No matter what that horse tells you...he never won the Kentucky Derby."

Q: How many Indianapolis Colts does it take to screw in a lightbulb?

A: Two...the other one recovers the fumble.

❅ ❆ ❅

Confucius say: Boxer who chews on foot gets sock in mouth.

❅ ❆ ❅

Pitcher: I thought I had pretty good stuff today.

Manager: The guys on the other team sure like it.

*They should move first base back a step to eliminate all the close plays.*

—John Lowenstein

*Although golf was originally restricted to wealthy, overweight Protestants, today it's open to anybody who owns hideous clothing.*

—Dave Barry

Hotel Guest: Does this place have a golf course?

Bell Captain: No.

Hotel Guest: Then why does the sheet on my bed have eighteen holes in it?

It was ten minutes until game time and fifteen miles from the stadium. Procrastinator Pete, the aging baseball manager of the home team, was speeding along the highway to get there. As luck would have it, Pete gets pulled over by the police. As the cop approaches the car, Pete rolls down his window.

The cop says, "Are you aware that you were speeding, sir?"

Pete replies, "Gee, no I wasn't, officer."

Pete's wife, who's riding shotgun, cackles, "Who are you kidding? You were going at least twenty miles an hour over the speed limit."

The cop peers down and says, "Uh, I see you're not wearing a seat belt."

Pete thinks quickly and says, "When you pulled me over, I thought I was going to have to get out of the car so I unfastened it."

His wife chimes in again. "That's a joke. You never wear a seat belt."

With that, the cop pokes his head in the driver's side window and says to Pete's wife, "Excuse me, ma'am, but does your husband always lie like this?"

She replies, "Nope...only when he's had too much to drink."

*A friend gave me seats to the World Series.*

*From where I sat, the game was just a rumor.*

—Henny Youngman

They've just invented a microwave television. Now you can watch a three hour baseball game in four minutes.

❄ ❄ ❄

Molly: My husband has a World Series ring, a Super Bowl ring, and an Olympic Gold Medal.

Polly: Boy, he must be a great athlete.

Molly: No...he owns a pawn shop.

Q: What's the difference between a football and
   Prince Charles?

A: One's thrown to the air, the other heir to the
   throne.

❄ ❄ ❄

Ralph was playing table tennis with a guy who
had a super duper slam shot. In a freak
accident, one such shot rammed right down
Ralph's mouth. He was rushed to the hospital,
given a local anesthetic and then the doctor began
to perform surgery.

First he cut into Ralph's left side, then his right,
then up into his chest and down into his belly.

Ralph shrieked, "Doc, why all the incisions!?!"

"That's just the way the ball bounces."

*I play in the low 80's. If it's any hotter*
*than that, I won't play.*

—Joe E. Lewis, on golf

*You win some, lose some, and wreck some.*

—Race car driver Dale Earnhardt

After Dallas Cowboys owner Jerry Jones dies and goes to heaven, God is taking him on a tour of the place. He shows Jerry a small three-bedroom home with a tiny Cowboys pennant hanging over the front porch.

"This is your eternal home, Jerry," says God. "You should feel mighty proud because most folks don't get their own private living quarters here."

Jerry looks at the home, then does an about face and sees this huge four-story mansion with two gigantic Oakland Raiders flags flying between the four marble pillars. And parked in the circular driveway is a black and silver limo with the Raiders logo on the hood.

"Thanks for my home, God," says Jerry, "but I have just one question. You give me this tiny home with a miniature Cowboys pennant and Al Davis gets that beautiful mansion. How come?

God laughs and says, "Oh, that's not Al Davis' home. That's mine."